Gary Jones

London

First published by Gary Jones in 2016.

Copyright © Gary Jones, 2016.

All rights reserved. No part of this publication may be reproduced, stored, or transmitted in any form or by any means, electronic, mechanical, photocopying, recording, scanning, or otherwise without written permission from the publisher. It is illegal to copy this book, post it to a website, or distribute it by any others means without permission.

This book was professionally typeset on Reedsy.
Find out more at reedsy.com

Contents

Introduction	1
Crash Course on the History of London	4
Transport	12
Hotels	18
London's Best Museums	21
Art in London	35
Historical Places	42
Cosmopolitan London	50
Shopping	54
Music	62
Top 5 London Restaurants	65
Parks	68
Only in London	72
London's Best Bars and Pubs	74
Night Clubs	80
London in 3 Days	82
Conclusion	85

1

Introduction

This guide was designed for people with limited time in London and who want to get the most out of their short stay. This is not a long book about everything in London. This book is the London essentials.

London is an amazing city and has a rich history that stretches back for two millennia.Today London is a trendsetting global city and have great experiences to offer visitors.London is a city of diversities, old mixed with new.On London streets, you will find people from all over the world that live and work in London.It's a true global city.

If you have limited time in London, then my advice to you is not to try and see everything.Rather go to the best London has to offer and leave the rest for another trip.London will be a great experience if you take your time and truly experience the best the city has to offer.Don't spend 5 minutes in every attraction in London and never really experience the energy of London.

This book will give you a good glimpse and idea of what London has to offer.

Despite all the landmarks, structures and testament to its ancient roots, London is a highly urban place, dotted with history. From the Tower of London and similar buildings to the modern clubs and restaurants, experience the mingling of the ancient and the modern, all in one harmonious symphony.

I wrote this book with a limited time frame in mind. Go see the best of London and spend some quality time there. This way you will really experience this amazing city and have memories you can carry with you forever.

I hope you have a great time in London!
Good Luck!

2

Crash Course on the History of London

London is the place where history was made. It has witnessed the rise and fall of empires, families, leaders, tyrants, and politicians. It also became home to artists and scientists alike. With its long history, London might just have seen it all.

The city's name originated from a Celtic word- Londinios- meaning "where the bold one is". In 43 AD, the Romans invaded Britain and then built a bridge across the River Thames. Later, the Romans realized the attractive possibility of building a port in the place. It was perfectly situated; it was far away inland from Germanic raiders, but the water was still deep enough for large ships to come in.

London quickly became the largest British town. It became a typical Roman city, with a forum in the center, amphitheaters and numerous bathhouses.

During the Dark Ages, London ceased to be a town. The walls were still intact, but only a few people lived within the town. After a few years, it rose from obscurity. The new town was much smaller. The town soon became a bustling location where ships from all over Europe landed. By the early 8th century, London became a trading center.

The Danes looted London in 842, and later conquered the rest of Northern and Eastern parts of England. In 878, King Alfred the Great defeated the invading Danes. England was divided, and London remained under the Danes. King Alfred took London back in 886 and repaired the old Roman walls. The entire town returned to its original state and became a flourishing town once more.

London Bridge is falling down...

The popular children's rhyme is believed to be a historical fact. It was believed to happen in the early parts of the 11th century. The king of Norway, King Olaf, attacked England. His men found it difficult to sail up the River Thames and past the London Bridge. King Olaf had his men sail to the London Bridge, the boats protected by wicker and wood canopies.

Once the boats were under the bridge, the men sailed close to the bridge's wooden struts and tied ropes around them. They rowed the boats away from the bridge, pulling the supporting struts, which caused the bridge to collapse.

London during the Middle Ages

During the Middle Ages, some of the most famous London structures were built. In 1066, London had a charter that confirmed certain rights to its town and citizens. The charter was given by William the Conqueror. From 1078 to 1100, a stone tower was built to replace the wooden one built by William, which stood guard over the town of London. This stone tower was the ancestor of what would later become the infamous Tower of London.

A stone bridge was built in 1176. This replaced the older wooden one that spanned the Thames River. In 1180, London was described as a happy, thriving town, with clean air. The people enjoyed religious contentment, with strong fortifications that protected them.

London during the 16th and 17th Century

Prosperity continued during these periods. More lands opened up for new buildings and new suburban areas that accommodated the increasing London population. London continued to expand until in 1600, the town is connected to the Westminster Palace through a row of houses.

In 1622, the Banqueting House was built. Hyde Park was opened to the public by the king in 1635. Richmond Park was created in 1637, which served as a hunting ground for Charles I and his court. Greenwich, which was near the flourishing London town, became the site for the building of the Queen's House in 1637.

In 1571, the Royal Exchange opened. It catered to the growing and bustling trade. Wool was London's main export. There were also several other trade goods such as rabbits' and sheep' skins, tin, lead and a myriad of spices and herbs.

The growth and progress of London continued despite the bubonic plague. Outbreaks occurred in 1603, and again in 1633 and 1665. After each outbreak, London's population was able to quickly recover.

During the rest of the 17th century, several civil wars and rebellions occurred. Then, in 1666, the great London fire occurred. The fire started small in a baker's house located in Pudding Lane, but because of the wind, it soon spread. It destroyed about 13,200 houses, leaving about 70,000 to 80,000 people homeless. Because of this disaster, the king ordered that all houses built in London should be made of brick and stone. St. Paul's was also a casualty of this fire. Rebuilding efforts started in 1675 and was finished in 1711.

London during the 18th century

Rapid population growth happened from the late 17th century to the 18th century. Hospitals were built during this period, such as Westminster in 1720, Guys in 1724, St Georges in 1733, London in 1740 and Middlesex in 1745.

In 1703, the famous Buckingham Palace was constructed for the equally famous Duke of Buckingham. John Nash altered the palace in the 10th century. In 1837, the first monarch to ever live in this palace was Queen Victoria.

Other notable establishments built during this period were:
- Marlborough House in 1711
- British Museum in 1753
- Mansion House in 175e, built to serve as the Lord Mayor of London's residence

- Houses built on the London Bridge were demolished in 1757
- Walls surrounding the city were demolished in 1760 to 1766
- New bridge built in Westminster in 1749
- Blackfriar's bridge built in 1770
- Somerset House built by Sir William Chambers in 1176-1786

London during the 19th century

The main activity in London during this time is expansion. One of the major reasons for this growth was the establishment of the railway system. In 1837, Euston Station was established. In 1852, the famous Kings Cross Station was constructed. The St Pancras' Station was constructed in 1868.

Other notable events in the 19th century were:
- In 1863, London witnessed the opening of the 1st underground railway system. Steam trains pulled the 1st carriages
- Train system ran on electricity, started on 1890 and became fully

electric in 1905
- Thames Tunnel was constructed in 1843.
- Parliament burned down in 1834, which Charles Barry rebuilt and included the now famous Big Ben clock tower.
- Trafalgar Square was created in 1839, with the Nelsons column built in 1842.
- Regents Park was opened to the public in 1838.
- Victoria Park was opened to the public in 1845
- Battersea Park was opened in 1858.
- Albert Hall, one of London's great landmarks was constructed in 1871.
- Museums opened such as Victoria & Albert Museum (more popularly referred to as the V & A) in 1852, Science Museum in 1857 and Natural History Museum in 1881.
- In 1891, The New Scotland Yard was constructed.
- In 1892, Piccadilly Square's statue of Eros was built

London during the 20th century

Early 20th century saw the continuation of progress in London. More structures were built such as:
- Westminster Cathedral in 1903
- V & A Museum moved in 1909 to where it is located today
- Geological Museum in 1935
- White City Stadium in 1908
- Wembley Stadium in 1923
- Gunnersbury Park in 1925
- Chiswick Bridge in 1933

Progress halted in World War II. London experienced huge losses. In September 1940, the Blitz began and more and more Londoners started sleeping in the city's underground stations. About 20,000 people died, and 25,000 were injured during this period.

After the war, London slowly got back to its feet. The city reconstructed what the war damaged. It even built some more:
- In 1945, the Waterloo Bridge was constructed.
- In 1951, the Royal Festival Hall was constructed.
- In 1956, the opening of the Pollock's Toy Museum took place.
- In 1962, the Shell Center opened.
- In 1963, the Millbank Tower was erected.
- In 1966, the Post Office Tower was opened, which quickly became one of the famous London landmarks.
- In 1968, opening of the Hayward's Gallery
- In 1976, opening of the Museum of London
- In 1979, opening of the Museum of Garden History
- In 1980, opening of the London Transport Museum
- In 1988, opening of the Museum of the Moving Image
- In 2000, the Somerset House was opened to the public.

London during the 21st century

London's growth continued rapidly at the start of the 21st century. There were many more sights and landmarks constructed and opened to the public:
- In 2000, the London Eye was opened to the public.
- In 2012, the Shard was opened.
- In 2012, Olympics was held in London, which confirmed its status as one of the greatest cities in the world.

Today, London's population is around 8.1 million. Many industries were founded and flourished in London, but the greatest as of today is tourism. Each year, millions of tourists come to the city to experience its long-standing history. The city's greatest attractions are the many landmarks and structures that were constructed over the centuries.

3

Transport

There are several ways to get from Heathrow Airport to London.If you are looking for a fast and easy way, then I recommend taking

TRANSPORT

the Heathrow Express. It will take about 15 minutes from Heathrow to Paddington station. At Paddington Station, you can take the subway or taxi. (The Subway is called the Tube or Underground in London) The Heathrow Express runs every 15 minutes.

Heathrow Express Website
https://www.heathrowexpress.com/
Phone: +44 (0) 345 600 1515

Heathrow Website
http://www.heathrow.com/
Heathrow Map
https://goo.gl/maps/FoPu6N2rYtM2

If you are looking for a cheap way from Heathrow, then take the subway from the airport. The subway trip will take about 1 hour to central London.

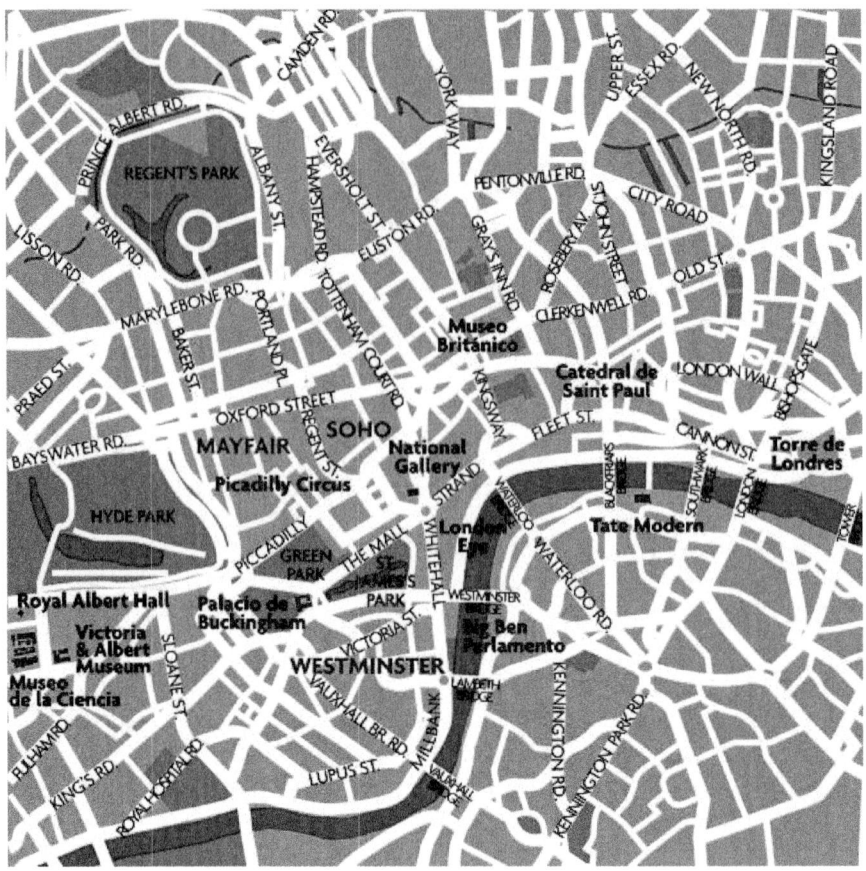

Subway(Underground or Tube)

Once in London the City subway system is very efficient and runs all over the city.To make your journey in London as convenient as possible buy an Oyster card.An Oyster card is an electronic card you can load up with cash or load with a weekly ticket.To make your transport in the city cheap and easy, I suggest you get a weekly ticket loaded up on your Oyster card.You can choose which Zones on the London underground you want your ticket to cover.The more Zones you cover, the more expensive.

London Underground Website
https://tfl.gov.uk/
Phone: 0343 222 1234

Buses

The London bus system can take you all over the city and easy to navigate. You can use your Oyster card to travel on all the city buses.

There are night buses that run after the subway closes that can take you back to the area you came from.

Taxis

If you want to take a taxi, then I suggest taking the traditional London black cabs. They all have the same unusual shape and can take up to 6 passengers. Inside you will notice the taxi driver ID and taxi number.

These taxis are safe and reliable. There is a cheaper option like minicabs, but they are not always reliable and not always safe especially when you travel alone, and it's late at night. The city regulates the traditional black cabs. The minicabs are just normal looking cars and sometimes have no recognizable sign that it's a taxi.

Taxis
https://tfl.gov.uk/modes/taxis-and-minicabs/book-a-taxi
Phone : 0871 871 8710
Thames River Bus

The Thames river bus is a great way to get around the city and see the amazing London attractions. These boats are faster than the normal river tour boats and will get you around the city fast. Refreshments and Wi-Fi are available on the boat. Tickets can be purchased at the pier ticket office.

Thames River Bus Website

TRANSPORT

https://tfl.gov.uk/modes/river/about-river-bus
Phone:020 7001 2200

4

Hotels

London is one of the most expensive cities in the world.So finding a good affordable hotel for your stay could be tricky, but I made a short list of some the best budget hotels in London.

Gloucester Place Hotel

Marylebone is one of the best areas in London, and you will be extremely central and walking distance to Oxford Street and Hyde Park. The hotel has traditional Georgian Style, and you will enjoy a very nice breakfast. The location is fantastic, and you can walk to Marble Arch Tube Station(subway) and Bond Street Tube Station. The legendary Madame Tussaud Museum is a 10-minute walk, and so is the Sherlock Holmes Museum in Baker Street.

Address: Gloucester Place Hotel, 55 -53 Gloucester Place,
Near Harley Street, London W1U 6AT
Phone: 020 7486 6166
Gloucester Place Hotel Website
http://www.gloucesterplacehotel.com/
Gloucester Place Hotel Map
https://goo.gl/maps/4cgnW9XqFkE2

Chiswick Court Hotel

If you want to stay outside the hustle and bustle of central London, then the Chiswick Court Hotel is perfect for you. Chiswick is one of the best areas in South West London and is a nice hideaway from all the tourist spots. The hotel is close to Turnham Green subway station.

Address: 39 Bath Rd, London W4 1LJ
Phone: 020 8995 9903
Chiswick Court Hotel Website
http://www.chiswickcourthotel.co.uk/
Chiswick Court Hotel Map
https://goo.gl/maps/2ZLVR77qtS62

Jesmond Hotel

The Jesmond Hotel is located in Bloomsbury and is also has the classic Georgian style. The hotel is close to Goodge Street Tube Station. One of the best things of this hotel is the lovely garden in the back where you can relax after a long day in the city.

Address: 63 Gower St, London WC1E 6HJ
Phone: 020 7636 3199
Jesmond Hotel Website
https://www.jesmondhotel.org.uk/
Jesmond Hotel Map
https://goo.gl/maps/J9xqUfiQjqM2

Tune Hotel

If you don't really care about staying in a traditional English Hotel, and you would rather stay in a simple modern bed and breakfast with no thrills, then book a room at the Tune Hotel. The Tune Hotel is in the Paddington area so you can take the Heathrow Express train straight to Paddington and get in and out of London in a very convenient way.

Address: 41 Praed St, London W2 1NR
Phone: 020 7258 3140
Tune Hotel Website
http://www.tunehotels.com/gb/en
Tune Hotel Map
https://goo.gl/maps/q9DCvTnFZxP2

5

London's Best Museums

What better way to see London's history and get a glimpse of its culture than by going to museums. There are numerous museums in and around the city. The best part about these museums, aside from their easy accessibility and wealth of history, is that most of them have free admissions.

The British Museum

This is London's, and among the world's, oldest museums. Located at 44 Great Russell Street, admission is free. Sometimes, there are admission charges for some of their temporary exhibitions.

The British Museum contains millions of objects. The collection is so vast that they can only be placed on display in batches. Tourists often make a beeline for certain popular exhibits like the Rosetta Stone, Lewis Chessmen, collection of mummies, the Sutton Hoo ship burial, and the Lindow Man.

The Sutton Hoo ship burial is the centerpiece of the recently opened Sir Paul and Lady Jill Ruddock Gallery. The display includes different finds across Europe, which dates back as early as AD 300 to 1100. In this exhibit, one can see the iconic Sutton Hoo masked helmet of the

Anglo-Saxons. There are also mosaics that date back to the late Roman era.

Some of the many amazing objects include the Lycurgus Cup (dating back to the 4th century, which was extraordinarily designed to change its colors when exposed to different lights) and the remarkable Kells Crozier (9th century holy staff made from yew wood, decorated and modified through the years).

There are also some permanent exhibitions like:
- Enlightenment: Exhibit that covers the 18th century. It also showcases thousands of objects, some of which from the mid-18th century to the early parts of the 19th century. There is also the former King's Library, which was recently restored. It contained George III's book collection.
- Living & Dying: Permanent in the Wellcome Trust Gallery. The exhibit explores the different diseases diagnosed and treated throughout the course of history. It also dealt with how people across the centuries coped with death, including the different rituals on mourning, festivals for the dead and burial.

Address: Great Russell St, London WC1B 3DG
Phone: 020 7323 8299
British Museum Website
http://www.britishmuseum.org/
British Museum Map
https://goo.gl/maps/EY9m6XL7pYG2

The V & A (Victoria and Albert Museum)
This is another of London's most notable museums that visitors must see. It is located in Knightsbridge and admission is free. The V &

A is among the most magnificent museums in the entire world. The foundation stone of the museum was laid by Queen Victoria herself in 1899, which was also her last official engagement in public.

The museum has a marvelous display of applied arts coming from all over the world. There are 150 grand galleries within its 7 floors. There are countless objects including various furniture, sculptures, ceramics, paintings, jewelry, glass, metalwork, dress, textiles and posters. All these are from various centuries. Most notable objects are:
- Raphael cartoons (7 in all), which were created in 1515. These were tapestry designs painted for the Sistine Chapel.
- A collection of sculptures during the Italian Renaissance, which are the most excellent in the category.
- Ardabil carpet, which is the oldest in the world and the most magnificent floor covering of all
- Jameel Gallery of Islamic Art

- Luck of Edenhall, which comes from Syria and is a 13th-century glass beaker
- Fashion galleries that showcase dresses ranging from 18th-century court dresses to contemporary chiffon ensemble
- Photography collection, famous for its more than 500,000 images
- Architecture Gallery, which houses numerous models, plans, descriptions and videos of various techniques

Address: Cromwell Rd, London SW7 2RL
Phone: 020 7942 2000
The V & A Website
http://www.vam.ac.uk/
The V & A Map
https://goo.gl/maps/2ahM36zB4nC2

The Natural History Museum

This famous museum is located along Gloucester Road. Admission is free. This astounding museum doubles as a research institution. The Natural History Museum opened in 1881, in the purpose built Palazzo of Alfred Waterhouse, which is in the Romanesque style. The NHM is now joined by the extension of the magnificent Darwin Center. The façade is in a magnificent pale blue and terracotta design.

Visitors are greeted by a Diplodocus skeleton, which takes up the entire length of the huge entrance hall. Going deeper inside the building will reveal the wonderful and exotic world of different creatures that roamed the earth then and now.

Address: Cromwell Rd, London SW7 5BD
Phone:020 7942 5000
Natural History Museum Website
http://www.nhm.ac.uk/
Natural History Museum Map
https://goo.gl/maps/WeWRQw48xJH2

The Science Museum

The Science Museum is in Knightsbridge and visitors are admitted for free. The museum has 7 floors that contain a wealth of entertaining and educational exhibits. One of the most notable exhibits is the command module of the famous Apollo 11. There is also a flight

simulator in the museum's exhibit. Other notable exhibits include:
- Wellcome Wing (developments in contemporary medicine, science, and technology)
- Medical History Gallery (collection of treasures in medical history)
- Pattern Pod (importance of patterns in modern-day science)
- Launch Pad (hands-on gallery that allows children to explore the basic principles of science)

Address: Exhibition Rd, London SW7 2DD
Phone: 0870 870 4868
Science Museum Website
http://www.sciencemuseum.org.uk/
Science Museum Map
https://goo.gl/maps/33bceEmEmMA2

Leighton House Museum
Similar to the Charles Dickens Museum, the Leighton House Museum was once the former home of Victorian artist Lord Frederic Leighton (1830 - 1896). It is a very fancy and remarkable infrastructure that was built during the 19th century. This house contains numerous paintings and sculptures that were crafted by Lord Leighton and his colleagues.

Leighton's place started out as a small house. But as he gained popularity, he embellished and extended his abode and turned it into a majestic palace of art. It boasts of the splendid Arab Hall, where your eyes will feast on a golden dome, elaborate mosaics, and walls that are lined with gorgeous Islamic tiles.

Lord's Leighton's vast painting studio, which is located on the upper floor, is one of the must-see sights for art lovers who are visiting London. It is filled with numerous paintings that are in their different stages of completion, and the walls are lined with his masterpieces. Popular figures from the Victorian age were given the chance to peruse inside the famous room. Queen Victoria, for instance, walked around these halls in 1859. The Leighton House Museum has different kinds of paintings in their collection.

They have 76 oil paintings that consist of the small, loosely-painted color sketches that Lord Leighton created as part of his picture-making process. Larger scale versions of these oil paintings can be found in the exhibition at the Royal Academy.

When it comes to sculpture, the famous artist has created three masterpieces. They may be few, but their influence over the new generation of British sculptors was massive in scale. The museum holds the three sculptures, which are – An Athlete Wrestling with a Python, The Sluggard, and Needless Alarms. The exhibit also has the plaster casts of the first sketch design for An Athlete Wrestling with a Python.

The biggest collection of this museum is Lord Leighton's drawings that are composed of 700 pieces of his sketches and studies. This collection was created to show his talent and skill as a draughtsman. The collection includes sketches from his younger years up to the time of his death.

Address: 12 Holland Park Rd, London W14 8LZ
Phone:+44 20 7602 3316
Leighton House Museum Website
https://www.rbkc.gov.uk/subsites/museums/leightonhousemuseum1.aspx
Leighton House Museum Map
https://goo.gl/maps/9GLBnbSpQE52

Charles Dickens Museum

At some point in our childhood, the famous author Charles Dickens has touched our lives with his beautiful literary masterpieces such as Oliver Twist, David Copperfield, Pickwick Papers, and A Tale of Two Cities. Now, you can relive the fun experience again and learn more about this great author at the Charles Dickens Museum.

This museum is located at 48 Doughty Street in the heart of Bloomsbury. This is also Charles Dicken's only surviving house in London. It was here where he finished Oliver Twist and started writing Nicholas Nickleby.

Visiting this house will provide you with a once in a lifetime opportunity to discover what would have been like when he was still living here, and learn more about his life and works.

Wandering through the rooms is like seeing how life and literature intertwine in perfect harmony. The author's old drawing room is filled with paintings, prints, and his reading desk, which gave birth to various beloved fictional characters.

The attic, on the other hand, shows the author's upheavals during his younger years and portrays them using several displays. There is a barred window from Marshalsea debtor's prison – the home of his family for years.

The entire museum holds 100,000 different other items including old manuscripts from his previous works, special editions, and some of his personal items. Each artifact is well preserved to maintain their beauty over the years.

In the house next door, there is a café where you can rest and have a little chat with fellow literary enthusiasts while sipping a cup of tea.

If you need to hold an event, the Charles Dickens Museum will be much happy to accommodate your needs. You can reserve some of its rooms when you want to conduct launch parties or business conferences. They have a very atmospheric and light environment that is ideal for a wide range of events.

Address: 48 Doughty St, London WC1N 2LX
Phone: 020 7405 2127
Charles Dickens Museum Website
http://dickensmuseum.com/
Charles Dickens Museum Map
https://goo.gl/maps/dKUrPrFhxxn

Grant Museum of Zoology

Aside from high fashion, art, and music, the United Kingdom is also well-known for its breakthroughs in scientific discoveries. The Grant Museum Zoology is the only remaining zoological museum in London. It boasts of a collection of more than 67,000 specimens that were collected from various species in the animal kingdom.

The museum was established in 1828 by Robert Edmond Grant. It was first used as a teaching collection for the University of London (now called University College London) which was also newly built at that time. In its 180 years of its existence, it has survived wars, flooding, and threats of closure.

The Grant Museum of Zoology is also considered as a "museum within a museum" because numerous collections from other local universities were transported here when they closed.

In here, you can see a collection of animal brains finely preserved in chemical fluids, collected specimens from expeditions such as Discovery, Challenger, and the Great Barrier Reef. There are also fossils of hominid materials, and also specimens of extinct or endangered animals like the Tasmanian Tiger, Quagga, giant deers, and the Dodo bird.

Aside from being a tourist attraction, this museum is also a great hub for knowledge. Researchers and scientists are warmly welcome to study here and peruse the full collection of the museum's specimens. Their collection includes a wide array of materials like fluid preserved species, pinned entomology, taxidermy, freeze-dried, and skeletal specimens.

Oftentimes, they also held special events in the museum. They will feature seminars, film showings, and even games or competitions. Most of these are free.

The Grant Museum of Zoology is open to the public every Monday to Saturday between 1 to 5 pm. If you want to conduct group and research visits, they are also open during the weekdays from 10 am to 1 pm. However, make sure that you book your reservations in advance.
Address:21 University St, London WC1E 6DE
Phone:020 3108 2052
Grant Museum of Zoology Website
http://www.ucl.ac.uk/museums/zoology
Grant Museum of Zoology Map
https://goo.gl/maps/uk41e161dyj

The National Maritime Museum

The National Maritime Museum in London is the largest Maritime Museum in the world. In this museum, you will experience the incredible stories of maritime exploration around the world. A visit to this museum is a remarkable experience.

The museum is located in Greenwich one of London's most historic areas. The museum is open daily 10am-5pm. Take a train Greenwich Station to get there.
Address: Park Row, Greenwich, London SE10 9NF
Phone: 020 8858 4422
The National Maritime Museum Website
http://www.rmg.co.uk/
The National Maritime Museum Map
https://goo.gl/maps/fNVqMgPwjxt

The Household Cavalry Museum

This military museum is unique in the sense that it will give you a behind the scenes look at the life of the Household Cavalry Regiment of the British Army.Visitors can take an inside look at the working stables of The Queen's Life Guard.The days to day life of the soldiers can be observed here.The tradition of the Queens Gaurd dates back 350 years. .To get there by subway go to Charing Cross station.The Museum is located in Whitehall and is a few minutes away from the subway station.

Address:The Household Division, Horse Guards, Whitehall, London SW1A 2AX
Phone:020 7930 3070
Household Cavalry Museum Website
http://www.householdcavalrymuseum.co.uk/
Household Cavalry Museum Map

LONDON

https://goo.gl/maps/URyZTCPv5jF2

6

Art in London

London, over the centuries, has been home to various artists. It has always supported grandmasters of the arts, as well as the obscure ones. Today, numerous art galleries pepper the city, exhibiting various art pieces from all over the world. The exhibits range from the classic to modern art.

Tate Modern

Admission is free in Tate Modern. This is among the top-ranking art galleries located in London. Tate Modern is considered in the art-world as a powerhouse for the modern art. The building is done in industrial architectural style. After all, the building was originally built as a power station after the Second World War. Sir Giles Gilbert Scott designed the original building, which was shut down in 1981.

Almost 20 years later, the former power station became a powerhouse that catered to modern art. Every year, about 5 million visitors marvel at the exhibits in Tate Modern. This huge visitor traffic prompted the highly ambitious expansion in 2012, which was called the Tanks. The name was in reference to the use of immensely cavernous old oil tanks. The Tanks is meant to hold film art and stage performances.

Large-scale installations are temporarily on display in the turbine hall, which is effective in lending awesome effects to the installations. There are also the permanent collections that consist of international modern art works from 1900 to present. The main galleries also permanently feature the works of the greats such as Beuys, Matisse and Rothko. All the artworks are expertly curated and grouped according to movement such as Post-war abstraction, Minimalist, Surrealism, etc.

Address:Bankside, London SE1 9TG
Phone:020 7887 8888
Tate Modern Website
http://www.tate.org.uk/visit/tate-modern
Tate Modern Map
https://goo.gl/maps/AaV3xN8dh8L2

The National Gallery

Located at the equally stunning Trafalgar Square, the National Museum is one of London's must-see art galleries. The gallery's collection of European paintings number to more than 2,000, ranging from works done from the Middle Ages up to the 20th century. Inspiring and awesome works of the masters like Leonardo da Vinci, Renoir, Van Gogh, Gainsborough, Rembrandt and Turner. Practically, all European schools of art are represented in the National Gallery's collection.

The gallery is divided in several exhibits housed in wings:
- Sainsbury Wing extension: earliest art works that the gallery owned like Italian paintings made by the early masters such as Piero Della Francesca and Giotto
- Sainsbury Wing basement: for temporary exhibitions

- West Wing: Italian Renaissance by Raphael, Titian, and Correggio
- North Wing: works by 17th century Italian, Flemish, Spanish and Dutch Old Masters
- East Wing: most popular paintings done by French Impressionists and post-Impressionists, such as the famous water lily paintings of Claude Monet and the sunflower series of Vincent Van Gogh

Address: Trafalgar Square, London WC2N 5DN
Phone:020 7747 2885
The National Gallery Website
http://www.nationalgallery.org.uk/
The National Gallery Map
https://goo.gl/maps/RCNWZbJrbtJ2

The ICA

The Institute of Contemporary Arts was originally founded to steer the art scene of the city towards a bolder and more daring new territory. This art gallery was a result of the collective efforts of various critics, artists, and poets in 1947. Most of the works here veer away from the laid-back themes of other schools of art. The collection is more on the rebellious kind of art.

Aside from the collections, the ICA also features cutting-edge bands, performance art, arthouse cinema performances, art-themed club nights and philosophical debates, among a few others that are meant to challenge accepted notions.

Address: The Mall, London SW1Y 5AH
Phone:020 7930 3647
The ICA Website
https://www.ica.org.uk/
The ICA Map
https://goo.gl/maps/y8VKULdFe7E2

The Barbican
This Barbican is a performing arts center and is one of the largest in Europe.The gallery hosts many art exhibitions and classical music concerts.The London Symphony Orchestra and the BBC Symphony

Orchestra are based in this gallery. To get to the Barbican by subway go to Barbican subway station.

Address: Silk St, London EC2Y 8DS
Phone: 020 7638 4141
The Barbican Map
https://goo.gl/maps/Rm6NmZ3iTM32

Somerset House

Somerset House has a collection of old masters and Impressionist and Post-impressionist paintings. This classical building that was constructed in 1776 hosts many rotating exhibitions that focus on art, design, fashion, and photography. To get there take the subway to Temple or Covent Garden stations.

Address: Strand, London WC2R 1LA

Phone:020 7845 4600
Somerset House Website
https://www.somersethouse.org.uk/
Somerset House Map
https://goo.gl/maps/cHj3NkEzNLn

The Royal Academy of Arts

The Royal Academy of Arts is is the oldest fine arts institution in Britain.The Academy is based in based in Burlington House on Piccadilly and was founded in 1768.The academy is special in the sense that it is an independent, privately funded institution led by eminent artists and architects.This unique situation gives it total artistic freedom.The Academy hosts some of the best temporary and touring exhibitions.To get there by subway go to Piccadilly Circus station.

Address: Burlington House, Piccadilly, London W1J 0BD
Phone:020 7300 8090
The Royal Academy of Arts Website
https://www.royalacademy.org.uk/
The Royal Academy of Arts Map
https://goo.gl/maps/Y6YXMTTxfX62

7

Historical Places

Buckingham Palace

A tour around London is not complete without stopping by at the Buckingham Palace. This tourist destination serves as a workplace and official London residence of the monarchy of the United Kingdom. This is one of the very few working royal palaces in the world. It is located in the City of Westminster.

The Buckingham Palace is mainly used by the Queen for official events and receptions. However, its State Rooms are open for public viewing every year. This grand palace is composed of 775 rooms. It has 19 State rooms, 52 Royal and guest bedrooms, 188 staff bedrooms, 92 offices, and 78 bathrooms.
The infrastructure measures 108 meters long across the front, 120 meters deep, and has a height of 24 meters.

This palace is furnished with numerous works of art that forms the Royal Collection, one of the largest art collections in the world, even though it is not an art gallery or a museum. These include work from Rembrandt, Rubens, and Canaletto.

Tourists who are planning to visit the Buckingham Palace will have a splendid time entering inside its grand halls. One of the most highly-recommended places to visit is the Windsor Castle, which houses the Great Kitchen. This is the oldest and the most substantially unchanged working kitchens in the country and has remained busy for 750 years.

The State Rooms, on the other hand, will show you a glimpse of the monarchy's history through art. Its gilded ceilings and glittering chandeliers make it a befitting location to place some of the Royal Collection's fine masterpieces.

In addition, you can also take a leisurely stroll in the palace garden. The best places to visit is the Herbaceous Border, the wisteria-clad summer house, the rose garden, and the Palace tennis court where King George VI and Fred Perry had a friendly match in the 1930s.

Address: London SW1A 1AA
Phone: 0303 123 7300

Buckingham Palace Website
https://www.royal.uk/
Buckingham Palace Map
https://goo.gl/maps/oz8ra9uoBCt

Tower of London

The colossal infrastructure that is the Tower of London is a prime example of Norman military architecture. Built by William the Conqueror on the Thames, this tower is created to protect London and ensure that his power will stay intact. It has a very rich layer of history and is considered as one of the most significant symbols of royalty.

There are various places and artifacts to visit in the Tower of London. The infrastructure is the keeper of the famous Crown Jewels. You will be able to see numerous artifacts that British monarchs have used over centuries such as the coronation spoon, sovereign's scepter with cross, St. Edward's crown, the imperial state crown, and the crown of Queen Elizabeth.

Another spectacle to view in the Tower of London is the Yeomen warders. Popularly known as the Beefeaters, they have been guarding the tower for centuries and their origins stretch back as far as Edward IV's reign. You can talk to modern day Yeomen warders and discover tales about intrigue, torture, execution, and a whole lot more.

Other activities that you can try are spotting the legendary ravens around the tower, seeing the terrifying instruments of torture in the Wakefield Tower, and the Fusilier Museum.

Address:London EC3N 4AB
Phone:0844 482 7777
Tower of London Website
http://www.hrp.org.uk/tower-of-london/
Tower of London Map
https://goo.gl/maps/1MELqoFC8Av

Extra Time
St Paul's Cathedral

St Paul's Cathedral is one of the most famous landmarks in London. The original church that was built on the same site dates back to 604AD. The current structure was built and finished in 1708. This Anglican Cathedral is the second biggest in England.

Address:St. Paul's Churchyard, London EC4M 8AD
Phone:020 7246 8350
St Paul's Cathedral Website
https://www.stpauls.co.uk/
St Paul's Cathedral Map
https://goo.gl/maps/eRhxaLCJEuv

Westminster Abbey
The spectacular church is a massive gothic style abbey chuch. This church plays a important part in the history of England and the United Kingdom. Westminster Abbey is the traditional place of coronation

and is also the burial site for English and, later, British royalty.

Address:20 Deans Yd, London SW1P 3PA
Phone:020 7222 5152
Westminster Abbey Website
http://www.westminster-abbey.org/
Westminster Abbey Map
https://goo.gl/maps/zrPhivawyp32

Houses of Parliament

The Palace of Westminster is also known as the Houses of Parliament and is the meeting place for the House of Commons and the House of Lords.The drama of British Politics happens between these walls.The Palace of Westminster was the main residence of the Kings of England until a fire destroyed much of the building in 1512.

Address:London SW1A 0AA
Phone:020 7219 3000
Houses of Parliament Website
http://www.parliament.uk/visiting/
Houses of Parliament Map
https://goo.gl/maps/PQamJtmVgG32

Kensington Palace

Kensington Palace is most famous for being the official residence of Princess Diana.It remained the official residence of the Princess after her divorce until her death. Kensington Palace has been an official residence of the British Royal Family since the 17th century.

HISTORICAL PLACES

Address:Kensington Gardens, London W8 4PX
Phone:020 3166 6000
Kensington Palace Website
http://www.hrp.org.uk/kensington-palace/#gs.cN1EkzI
Kensington Palace Map
https://goo.gl/maps/nGH232HF3su

8

Cosmopolitan London

London is a very cosmopolitan city and its a melting pot of cultures and nationalities. Let's take a look at a few interesting places in London.

Chinatown

If you wanted to visit a place where the oriental and western cultures blend together in harmony, then London's Chinatown is the best place for you.

The Chinese community of businesses and restaurants in London had a very long history dating back in the 18th century. The community started out in the city's East End side. The community's popularity bloomed in the 1950s, when British soldiers who came from the Far East discovered the rich and savory flavors of the Chinese cuisine. In the present times, the Chinese community has grown larger than before and is now located in the west of the Charring Cross road and is greatly concentrated on Gerard Street and Lisle Street.

If you are in Chinatown, one of the first things that should do is to fill your tummies with the most delicious oriental dishes. There's the Baozi Inn that offers spicy delicacies that are cheap yet flavorful, the Café TPT that boasts a wide menu of Hong Kong inspired dishes and good service, or the Four Seasons restaurant, which is popular for their

Cantonese-style roast duck. Whether you are looking for cheap meals or high-end restaurants, there is always a place in Chinatown that fits your budget.

In addition, you can also improve your cooking skills by trying to whip up your own Chinese dish. The New Loon Fung market is a large hive that sells oriental produce such as chrysanthemum tea, ginger, and spinach noodles.

Chinatown is best visited during January to February where the community celebrates the Chinese New Year. The dragon dances and the fireworks display are truly a sight to behold.

Address:55-57 Charing Cross Rd, London WC2H 0BL
Phone:020 7287 2220
Chinatown Website
http://www.chinatownlondon.org/
China Town Map
https://goo.gl/maps/DRePKN3BZct

Camden Town

Camden is another interesting area of London is seen as the main area of alternative culture in London.Walking down the streets of Camden will bring you into a mix of markets and music venues.

Camden is famous for arts, music and just being different.Camden is symbol of the cosmopolitan nature od London and is a melting pot of different elements in London finding expression through art and music.

Getting to Camden is easy with Camden Town subway station being close to all the markets and main attractions in the area.

The Camden Markets is something special and offers a wide variety of fashion, food , books and antiques.If you are looking for alternative goods then Camden is the place for you.

Camden Town Website
http://www.camdentown.co.uk/
Camden Town Map
https://goo.gl/maps/wefzUkhtvS12

Edgware Road

The Southern part of Edgware Road is well known for its diverse Middleastern and African cultural influence. If you love Middle Eastern Food then Edgware Road is the place for you. Late at night you will find many 24-hour kebab and shawarma restaurants.

To get to Edgware Road by subway, get off at the Edgware Road station.

Edgware Road Map

https://goo.gl/maps/FZ8edhiZkCr

9

Shopping

London is also the home of street fashion and couture thriving well side-by-side. Even the small street shops offer some incredible finds. The best shopping districts for different tastes include this short list:

Oxford Street
This is heart of the shopping experience in the city of London. Here, shoppers are greeted with over 300 different shops, including landmark stores and designer outlets. This is also where the renowned Selfridges is found.

All of the famous high end chains have their shops in Oxford Street, along with famous department store chains Debenhams and John Lewis. While in Oxford, one can easily slip into a side street to get out of the opulent shopping experience and into Berwick Street and St Christopher's Place among others for a few real treats.

Oxford Street Website
http://oxfordstreet.co.uk/
Oxford Street Map
https://goo.gl/maps/2kpG50i84go

Mayfair and Bond Street

This is where you can find people who wish to burn money, splurge on some high quality designer clothes or feast the eyes on luxurious items. This is also considered as London's exclusive shopping area where the rich and the celebrities go on shopping sprees. Shops include Tiffany & Co., Louis Vuitton and Burberry.

Mayfair Map
https://goo.gl/maps/9RbKPmGzr1C2

Carnaby Street
This is an iconic shopping district just 2 minutes away from the Piccadilly Circus and Oxford Circus. Carnaby Street gave birth to the

cultural and fashion revolution in the 60s. The iconic arch is a gateway to some historic shopping experience. Over 150 brands and more than 50 independent bars and restaurants can be found along this historic street. It also hosts a fascinating mix of heritage brands, stores, new designer names and independent boutiques.

Carnaby Street Website
http://www.carnaby.co.uk/
Carnaby Street Map
https://goo.gl/maps/jqVkY5EbCzP2

Covent Garden

This is the place to go for those who are looking for unique items, hip fashion, handmade one-of-a-kind jewelry or rare sweets. Neal Street offers funky cosmetics, latest urban streetwear and some funky unique shoes. Covent Garden Market is where interesting arts and crafts are found. Distinctive London shopping experience can also be experienced along St Martin's Courtyard, Seven Dials, Shorts Gardens, Neal's Yard, Monmouth Street and Floral Street.

Covent Garden Website
https://www.coventgarden.london/#
Covent Garden Map
https://goo.gl/maps/fFWrvPecp8q

King's Road
Shopping is the main obsession in this place. Shoppers are treated to unique labels, high-street labels, designer shops and trendy boutiques. Vivienne Westwood's Shop is found here, which gave birth to punk fashion in the 70s.

King's Road Map
https://goo.gl/maps/1CK1aMfB74u

Knight's Bridge
Knightsbridge and Brompton Road is the go-to place of visitors all over the world looking to shop illustrious brands. Harvey Nichols and

Harrods are located here, along with other shops that offer the latest trends.

Knight's Bridge Map
https://goo.gl/maps/xg1GLy66BQp

Notting Hill

This was made famous by a Hollywood movie of the same name. Quite a number of small and unique shops are located here. Visitors find vintage clothing, unusual fashion items, organic food, unique books, quirky gifts and rare antiques.

Notting Hill Website
http://www.thehill.co.uk/
Notting Hill Map
https://goo.gl/maps/v66MXdTdGNP2

Markets in London

If you are looking for some interesting items to buy in West London, the Portobello Road Market is the perfect place for you. It is a very popular street market for locals and tourists alike. Hundreds of stalls filled with cheap trinkets, clothes, accessories, food, and souvenirs pile up along the two mile stretch of the Portobello road. It is usually busy during weekends, especially Saturday afternoons.

The Portobello Road Market started as a winding country path known as the Green Lane. In the 1850s, the marketplace started to take shape to accommodate families living in newly developed homes in Paddington and Notting Hill. From simple antiques to second-hand household items, the market expanded and expanded until it developed into what it is today.

The street market is divided into distinct sections. There is the antique's section that stretches from the Chepstow Villas to Eigin Crescent. From Eigin Crescent to Talbot Road, you will find stalls filled with fruits and vegetables. For cheap socks, laundry bags, and other everyday goods, visit the Westway.

Fashionable clothes and accessories can also be found on Westway, but other stalls are also scattered along the general side of the street. For second hand goods, the road from Westway to Golborne Road is lined up with stalls that sell these items.

Aside from shopping, there are also fun activities that one can do when visiting Portobello Road Market. There's the electric cinema where you can watch old and new movies while sitting comfortably in plush armchairs or two seat sofa. The Noting Hill Carnival, meanwhile, is a large street festival that is held every year during the August Bank Holiday.

Portobello Road Market Website
http://shopportobello.co.uk/
Portobello Road Market Map
https://goo.gl/maps/k94baiMZL032

Billingsgate Market
The United Kingdom is one of the best producers of the freshest and richest sea delicacies in the world. The Billingsgate market is a hub for fish enthusiasts to see all the most delicious underwater ingredients that the country has to offer.

As the country's largest inland fish market, it sells 25,000 tonnes of fish and other underwater products each year. In addition, 40% of the products sold were imported from abroad. The annual turnover rate of the market can reach up to £200 million.

SHOPPING

Billingsgate Market covers a vast land that measures up to 13 acres and is totally self-contained. The main floor offers a large trading hall with 98 stands and 30 shops. These include cafes, a boiling room for shellfish, cold rooms, a freezer store, and an ice making plant. You can also meet catering suppliers and merchants that specialize in poultry, non-perishable products, and other services.

Almost every port in the United Kingdom delivers their goods to this market. Once the fishes reach the coast, they are transported by road and arrive on the market during the early hours of the morning. The imported goods are sent using through large refrigerated containers to maintain its freshness. Live imports such as lobsters or eels come from Canada and even as far away as New Zealand.

There is also several processed seafood that is on display. These include cured or smoked fish and roe, as well as prepared meals like fish soup, cooked shellfish, and pâtés.

If you wanted to learn the proper ways of cooking delectable seafood, you can also in the Billingsgate Seafood Training School. It offers several courses on fish recognition, knife skills, food presentation, cooking, as well as nutrition. It is located in the heart of the market.

The Billingsgate Market is open on Tuesday to Saturday. Trading begins at 5 a.m. to 8:30 p.m.

Billingsgate Market Website
http://www.billingsgate-market.org.uk/
Billingsgate Market Map
https://goo.gl/maps/BX5Db3Z5JQE2

10

Music

West End Musicals

Experience the glitz and glamour of the theater by checking out the musical performances in the West End side of London.

The west end theaters are never quiet. Every night, the infrastructures are glowing with bright neon lights that signal and are filled with posters of the next main, theatrical attraction.

Most of the theater houses here are of late Victorian and Edwardian construction giving them a very classic yet elegant feel.

The West End stages are also home to the longest running musical performances such as Cats, Blood Brothers, The Phantom of the Opera, Jesus Christ Superstar, Lion King, and a whole lot more. If you wanted to see the best of London's culture and performing arts scene, the West end theaters are the most highly-recommended places to visit.

Email: customerservices@londontheatre.co.uk
Phone: +44 (0) 20 7492 0810
West End Musicals Website
https://www.londontheatre.co.uk/whats-on/musicals

Royal Opera House

The Royal Opera House is one of the finest opera houses and major performing arts venue in the United Kingdom. It is located in Covent

Garden, central London. It is the home of the Royal Ballet, the Royal Opera, and the Royal Opera House Orchestra.

There are available guided tours, exhibitions, and fine displays of art to relish and look at.

The building itself has wide open space that will make you feel relaxed and comfortable. It is a perfect getaway from the hustle and bustle of the city.

There are many places that you can visit at the Royal opera House. The first is the Paul Hamlyn Hall. It is a mini crystal palace that was built using Victorian style engineering and ironwork. It used to be a flower market and a concert hall. But now, it is a hall that showcases costumes and other artifacts from previous plays.

The Crush Room, meanwhile, is home of the two popular divas in the 19th century – Australian soprano Dame Nellie Melba and the Italian coloratura soprano Adelina Patti. Their beautiful bust sculpture is located in this room.

If you feel a little bit famished, the Amphitheater Bar is just around the corner. Paintings from popular modern and contemporary artists line its walls, which will surely provide excitement to every art lover out there.

In addition, the amphitheater bar has a majestic terrace where you can view the London skyline. Here, you can see the London's Eye, Nelson's Column, Westminster's Cathedral, Waterloo Station, and numerous infrastructures from a distance.

The Royal Opera House is open daily from people who want to learn more about art and culture. From Mondays to Saturdays between 10 am and 3 pm, bars and restaurants in the venue are also open to accommodate customers.

Address:Bow St, London WC2E 9DD
Phone:+44 (0)20 7304 4000
Royal Opera House Website
http://www.roh.org.uk/
Royal Opera House Map
https://goo.gl/maps/Xa94sSGeXRM2

11

Top 5 London Restaurants

TOP 5 LONDON RESTAURANTS

London is a great place for food lovers and those looking for food adventure. Street foods abound, with amazing flavors and great textures. There are the ever-present fish-and-chips on every corner and in every street. Aside from these, there are numerous budget-friendly restaurants that offer amazing food.

Dinner (Heston Blumenthal)

This is a light-filled restaurant located at the Mandarin Oriental. It is best known for its reinterpretation of British historic dishes, such as the Salmagundi of the 18th century (chicken, marrow bone and salsify) and the Taffety Tart (rose, apple, blackcurrant and fennel sorbet). Aside from great food, service and stories, the view of Hyde Park is definitely a great add-on.

Address: Mandarin Oriental Hyde Park
66 Knightsbridge,
London SW1X 7LA
Phone: +44(0)20 7201 3833
Dinner Website
http://www.dinnerbyheston.com/
Dinner Map
https://goo.gl/maps/r4fDsihp7Gy

Coq d'Argent

This restaurant, Brasserie and bar is located at the rooftop of the pink-and-terracotta James Stirling building. During the week, the restaurant serves classic French cuisine. On the weekends, the atmosphere is relaxed with jazz music and a brunch menu.

Address:The Poultry, 1 Poultry, London EC2R 8EJ
Phone: 020 7395 5000
Coq d'Argent Website
http://www.coqdargent.co.uk/
Coq d'Argent Map
https://goo.gl/maps/ZAuLtC8c9Nu

Bonds

The Bonds also doubles as an in-house dining for Threadneedles. It also has a separate entrance, which caters to a majority of traders and bankers, especially on Thursdays and Fridays.

The menu is modern European fare with an Asian twist. The interior also incorporates a few Asian accents, like exotic flowers and sleek wood. Bonds is rated as one of the hotels that offer best value in London.

Address:5 Threadneedle St, London EC2R 8AY
Phone: 020 7657 8144
Bonds Website
https://www.hotelthreadneedles.co.uk/food-and-drink/Breakfast
Bonds Map
https://goo.gl/maps/RrsP36g5kS42

Sweetings

This establishment is a reminder of the time when London was a place swarming with chaps wearing pinstripe suits and carried furled umbrellas. Sweetings is a 120-year-old restaurant that specializes in fish and seafood.

Address:39 Queen Victoria St, London EC4N 4SF
Phone: 020 7248 3062
Sweetings Website
http://www.sweetingsrestaurant.co.uk/
Sweetings Map
https://goo.gl/maps/QCxTiKRd4NJ2

Kitchen W8

This is one of London's sleek neighborhood restaurant, which opened in 2009. The interior is all smooth chairs and very sophisticated, with an atmosphere of "café au lait-bitter chocolate" type with a banquet seating. It is an opulent place to dine, which earned it a Michelin star in 2011. It was described as a place where English food is served with a French soul. It balances out its sophistication with a relaxed dining experience, BYO-style on Sunday evenings and set menus at great values.

Address:11-13 Abingdon Rd, London W8 6AH
Phone:020 7937 0120
Kitchen W8 Website
http://www.kitchenw8.com/
Kitchen W8 Map
https://goo.gl/maps/MNgS9yCzijR2

12

Parks

One of the greatest things of London is the amazing parks all over the city.If you are staying in London for a few days, make sure to visit a few parks.Here is a list of my favorite parks in London:

Hyde Park

Hyde Park is probably the most famous park in London.The park is a famous venue for Music festivals and social gatherings.The park is Massive and is a favorite with cyclists, walkers and skaters.One of the famous landmarks in the park is the Princess Dianna Memorial Fountain.The park has almost 4000 trees and is a great place to relax and read a book.

Phone:0300 061 2000
Hype Park Website
https://www.royalparks.org.uk/parks/hyde-park
Hyde Park Map
https://goo.gl/maps/8Y6Z4fVxW5u

Richmond Park

Richmond Park is another massive park in London. The park is about 1,000 hectares. The park is famous for almost 600 deer walking freely in the park. The park has great views from the hill over the city.

Phone:0300 061 2200
Richmond Park Website
https://www.royalparks.org.uk/parks/richmond-park
Richmond Park Map
https://goo.gl/maps/6MwVW2S9Asx

Greenwich Park

Greenwich Park is the oldest Royal Park in London and offers some of the best views in London. The Royal Observatory is located in the park. This park is also great for relaxing and taking a break from the busy city life.

Phone:0300 061 2380
Greenwich Park Website
https://www.royalparks.org.uk/parks/greenwich-park
Greenwich Park Map
https://goo.gl/maps/Zd9XeucK7rH2

St James's Park
St James's Park is close to 3 royal palaces. This big park is famous for its lake and the pelicans that live in it. The Horse Guards Parade is also located in this park. The Household Cavalry, the British Army Regiment, is one of the Queens official Guard Regiments, and they can be observed in this park.

Phone:0300 061 2350
St James's Park Website
https://www.royalparks.org.uk/parks/st-jamess-park
St James's Park Map
https://goo.gl/maps/qAc3L8rEoVy

Clapham Common

Clapham Common is located in the south of London and is a great open space in the city.It's perfect for sports matches and is great social park for fun and games.The park has three ponds, tennis courts and grass pitches.If you want to have a great relaxing day with family and friends then visit Clapham Common.

Clapham Common Website
http://www.lambeth.gov.uk/places/clapham-common
Clapham Common Map
https://goo.gl/maps/KECUyconYvG2

13

Only in London

London is known for its one-of-a-kind take on everything- street fashion that veers off from the usual, high-end fashion that's truly unique and awe-inspiring, to the best beers and wonderful food. Aside from getting to experience modern urban living that bustles in a place with a rich ancient root, there are a few other things that visitors can experience only in London.

London is increasingly becoming popular for its pop-up events- whether a pop-up club, festival or restaurant. Pop-up is something that is set up in a few hours, makes a huge wave in the scene and then packs up when the sun goes up. Nobody ever really knows when they will see the club or restaurant again, or if they will get to see them again. This uncertainty makes the event even more exciting.

Popular
Kopparberg Urban Forest

This is a Critics' choice for pop-up club. This is a musical forest with a Scandinavian theme. It first landed in the summer of 2014, in Dalston. It has recently announced a comeback for 2015, over in Hackney Wick. The program is packed with DJ sets and numerous gigs. Event goers are treated to an array of street food and 2 bars.

E-mail: info@kopparbergurbanforest.com

Website

http://kopparbergurbanforest.com/

Night Tales
This is another Critics' Choice. Night Tales helped the London population to make it through arduous winters. It is an incredible pop-up party filled with street food and creative cocktails with DJs spinning party music in the background.
Address:1-2 Hepscott Road
London E9 5EN
Website
https://www.facebook.com/nighttalesLDN

Summer Tales
A spin-off of Night Tales held in summer. The party has a jungle theme, which runs for 15 weekends. True to the theme, there are numerous plush hammocks spread all over the party area, with rope swings and a terrace 20 meters wide where people can soak up the summer sun.
Website
http://www.nighttales.co.uk/

Rhythm Parlour
This is another Critics' Choice. This one-of-a-kind pop-up monthly event offers beard-trimming and haircut with disco bliss in the background. The Rhythm Parlour is happening in Rye Wax Records, inside Peckham's Bussey Building. Goers get treated to some trimming (hair, mustache or beard) by Ryan MacGregor and his team, with some cocktails, and music (house and funk). Definitely a true London-only experience.
Website
https://www.facebook.com/therhythmparlour

14

London's Best Bars and Pubs

London is one of the best places in the worlds to eat, drink, and be merry.Migrations, invasions and trade that span centuries have definitely influenced the food and bar scene in this old, yet modern city. There are just so many places to eat and drink that one can go to a different pub each day for a year and still not be able to go through all of them.

Difference Between a Pub and a bar?

Pubs are a very important part of British society.Going to a traditional Pub is one of those experiences that you have to have in London. British people love to be social, and there is no better place to grab beer after work with friends than a pub.

I often get asked what is the difference between a pub and a bar.The main difference between the two is that in a pub the atmosphere is more casual, and the food choices are usually better. It is common to have lunch or dinner in a pub, but not a bar. Bars will typically serve a wide variety of mixed drinks and liquors.For example, you might get cocktails at a bar, but not a pub.Pubs focus on a wide variety of beers and classic pub food.At a pub, you have to order food and drinks at the bar.Pubs do not offer table service.

Closing Hours:According to British law pubs close at 11 PM.You will hear the bell for last rounds at around 10:55 pm.

Bars have a different atmosphere than pubs. The music is louder, and the crowd is different.

Closing Hours:Most bars are open until 2 am because they have different rules, according to law.

Pubs

A visit to London won't be complete without a visit to some of the best traditional pubs in London.The pubs of the UK are unique and really gives you a sense of the great social dynamics in London.The pubs of London are where everybody from all walks of life gets together to have a pint of beer and talk about life.There are over 7000 pubs in London.I have picked out a few of the best traditional pubs in London.

Ye Old Mitre Tavern

This quaint old tavern is in Farrington, believed to be built in 1546 by Bishop Goodrich. This is a traditional tavern in every sense- cramped, 3-roof space, with stand-up tables in the enclosed courtyard out front. The tavern is accessible through alleyways branching from 2 separate streets.

The tavern offers ales with history:
- Caledonian 80
- George Gale Seafarers
- Adnams Broadside
- Deuchars IPA
- Fuller's Honeydew

There are also a few wines such as pinot grigio Veneto and pinot noir La Lumiere. Food is old-school pub such as:
- Pork pies
- Scotch eggs
- Toasted sandwiches
- And other full hearty meals

Address:1 Ely Pl, London EC1N 6SJ
Phone:020 7405 4751
Ye Old Mitre Tavern Website
http://www.yeoldemitreholborn.co.uk/
Ye Old Mitre Tavern Map
https://goo.gl/maps/TSEH43h3Rmt

The Viaduct Tavern

This pub is Located in the St Paul's area of London and is very central.It's located in a historic area and is opposite the Old Bailey.The pub is in a great area if you like to have a pint of beer in a historic area of London.The pub has a good variety of Ales on tap.This pub is a great place to drink a traditional English Gin and Tonic. The pub also has a good collection of wines. Th pub also serves traditional Engish pub food, from fish pie and beef stew to pie and mash.

Address:126 Newgate St, London EC1A 7AA
Phone:020 7600 1863
The Viaduct Tavern Website
http://www.viaducttavern.co.uk/
The Viaduct Tavern Map
https://goo.gl/maps/1PND4Bqroco

The George Inn

This pub is over 300 years old and is one of favorites to visit. This pub has an amazing atmosphere and is a great place for a party with friends or a leisurely Sunday pint of beer. The George has a fine variety of beer and food. The George Inn is South of the river and not very central but its well worth the trip. To get there by subway go to Southwark Station.

Address:The George Inn Yard, 77 Borough High St, Southwark, London SE1 1NH
Phone:020 7407 2056
The George Inn Website
https://www.nationaltrust.org.uk/george-inn
The George Inn Map
https://goo.gl/maps/fU9LrqtQtjJ2

The Lamb

This historic pub has a Victorian-style interior and is a great place to have a traditional pub experience in central London. The pub was build around 1729 and is has a great atmosphere. The pub serves a nice variety of traditional British pub food and has a good variety of Beer and Ale. The pub is located in central London in the Holborn area. To get there by subway go to Holborn Station.

Address:94 Lamb's Conduit Street
Bloomsbury London, WC1N 3Lz
Phone:0207 4050713
The Lamb Website
http://www.thelamblondon.com/
The Lamb Map
https://goo.gl/maps/CJEDx5v3U1q

The Trafalgar Tavern

The Trafalgar Tavern in Greenwich is a riverside pub in Greenwich that is extremely popular with a great atmosphere.The Location of the pub next to the river makes it a great place to spend a summer day with friends and family.It has a nice beer and food menu and is definitely a must see when you go to Greenwich.To get there by train go to the Cutty Sark DLR train station.It is a 10 min walk from the station.

Address:Park Row, London SE10 9NW
Phone:020 8858 2909
The Trafalgar Tavern Website
http://www.trafalgartavern.co.uk/
The Trafalgar Tavern Map
https://goo.gl/maps/XoUc4PQ9vDA2

Bars

The Beer Shop

Located in Nunhead, The Beer Shop is a popular watering hole among locals and tourists alike. It is a friendly bar that is also a shop. They have an extensive selection of different beers. The back counter of The Beer Shop dispenses 3 delicious draught beers. Notable are the pale ales, namely, citrusy Moor Top from Buxton Brewery and fruity and smooth Monacus by Northern Monk.

This watering hole also offers over 60 different ciders, porters and bottled beers. Most of these are from London brewers, whose beers all have succinctly clear tastes. Examples are the well-known Camden Town Hells and Brewdog. There are other beers like By The Horn's Sour to the People (sour-mash, burgundy-aged vintage beer) and the blended Ratchet artisan ale by Siren available in 750 mL bottles.

The Beer Shop is more like an extension of the locals' living rooms. Anyone can bring their takeaway food and the shop happily supplies the beer. Everything in the shop is also available for takeaway. Fancy having draught beer takeaway in 2-pint containers.

Address:40 Nunhead Green, London SE15 3QF
Phone:020 7732 5555
The Beer Shop Website
http://www.thebeershoplondon.co.uk/
The Beer Shop Map
https://goo.gl/maps/6PFrKu8Yrx12

15

Night Clubs

Let's take a look at the top clubs of London:

Ministry of Sound

The Ministry of Sound is one of the most popular British record labels and a big phenomenon in the dance music since ever since 1991.

For dancers and party goers, this venue located in Gaunt Street London provides the best sound system and music collection that will make your hips and entire body groove to the beat. Also, the club is illuminated by a dazzling light show that will make the music come alive.

The Ministry of Sound has five distinct rooms that you can explore. The 103 is the first room and is also known as the heart of the club. The Legendary Box, meanwhile, is the largest room in the club, this is also where the world's famous DJs gather and present their astonishing beats to partygoers.

The third room is the Baby Box. It is quite small compared to the other two venues, providing a more intimate party experience.

The Loft is the Ministry of Sound's newest lounge bar. This is an ideal place to catch up on the upcoming records labels and promoters before they even hit the music stores. Finally, there is the VIP lounge. It has private balconies where you can a splendid overlooking view of the headlining DJs. You only get access to this room through table bookings, DJs and their guest lists, providing a very exclusive and intimate feel.

Thanks to the latest refurbishments of the place, the Ministry of Sound now also boasts other amenities such as four bars, four dance floors, four DJ booths, and a new audiovisual specification.

Address:103 Gaunt St, London SE1 6DP
Phone:0870 060 0010
Ministry of Sound Website
http://www.ministryofsound.com/#a3Iht7LsPiMIXkBj.97
Ministry of Sound Map
https://goo.gl/maps/Q7JDzXMmzbz

Studio 338
Studio 338 is one of the best and most popular clubs in London.Firstly this is the biggest club in London, so it has a lot of space.What makes the club special is that it has an outside terrace for clubbers to dance.If it's a cold night, you have the option of dancing on the heated terrace or move inside to the other dance floor.Studio 338 is famous for hosting World-class house and techno DJs.

Address:338 Boord St, London SE10 0PF
Phone:020 8293 6669
Studio 338 Website
https://www.facebook.com/studio338?fref=ts
Studio 338 Map
https://goo.gl/maps/9pF247W5y3r

16

London in 3 Days

Itching to go to London? Try this 3-day sample itinerary to maximize the London experience:

Day 1:

Idea 1: Hop on the sightseeing bus to see all the iconic and historical landmarks such as the St. Paul's Cathedral. The ticket for the bus is valid for 24 hours. Visitors can hop on and off the bus throughout the validity of the ticket. Other sites to see for this tour are: grand London view from the Shard, the Tower of London, and the Tower Bridge. End the day with a show in London's West End.

Idea 2: Walk around the city and hop on a taxi to see: Trafalgar Square, witness the changing of the Guards at the Buckingham Palace, visit the Churchill War Rooms, go to the Big Ben and the Westminster Abbey. Take the London Eye and see the city change from its day view into its charming night scene.

Day 2:
Idea 1:Ride the London Eye and see the city by day, visit the Big Ben, the Houses of Parliament, the Westminster Abbey, National Gallery, the Buckingham Palace and the Piccadilly Circus

Idea 2: Visit theMuseum of London or the British Museum, St Paul's Cathedral, Covent Garden and, at the end of the day, see a show on West End.

Day 3
Idea 1: Visit 2 of the best museums in London such as the V&A, the

Natural History Museum or the Science Museum. Do some shopping at Harrods and end the entire tour with a grand show at the Royal Albert Hall or The O2.

Idea 2: Visit the Tower Bridge, Tower of London, the Shard, HMS Belfast, Tate Modern. Then drop by Shakespeare's Globe Theater and end the tour with a treat at the Royal Festival Hall.

17

Conclusion

I want to thank you for reading this book! I sincerely hope that you received value from it!

Ó Copyright 2015 by Gary Jones - All rights reserved.
This document is geared towards providing exact and reliable information in regards to the topic and issue covered. The publication is sold with the idea that the publisher is not required to render accounting, officially permitted, or otherwise, qualified services. If advice is necessary, legal or professional, a practiced individual in the profession should be ordered.

- From a Declaration of Principles which was accepted and approved equally by a Committee of the American Bar Association and a Committee of Publishers and Associations.

In no way is it legal to reproduce, duplicate, or transmit any part of this document in either electronic means or in printed format. Recording of this publication is strictly prohibited and any storage of this document is not allowed unless with written permission from the publisher. All rights reserved.

The information provided herein is stated to be truthful and consistent, in that any liability, in terms of inattention or otherwise, by any usage or abuse of any policies, processes, or directions contained within is the solitary and utter responsibility of the recipient reader.

Under no circumstances will any legal responsibility or blame be held against the publisher for any reparation, damages, or monetary loss due to the information herein, either directly or indirectly.

Respective authors own all copyrights not held by the publisher.

The information herein is offered for informational purposes solely, and is universal as so. The presentation of the information is without contract or any type of guarantee assurance.

The trademarks that are used are without any consent, and the publication of the trademark is without permission or backing by the trademark owner. All trademarks and brands within this book are for clarifying purposes only and are the owned by the owners themselves, not affiliated with this document.

Printed in Great Britain
by Amazon